Exploring
SOUTH AMERICA

Rose Blue and Corinne J. Naden

Chicago, Illinois

For information, address the publisher:
Raintree
100 N. LaSalle, Suite 1200
Chicago IL 60602

Printed and bound in the United States.

08 07 06 05 04
10 9 8 7 6 5 4 3 2 1

Library of Congress Cataloging-in-Publication Data:
Blue, Rose.
  Exploring South America / Rose Blue and Corinne
J. Naden.
     v. cm. -- (Exploring the Americas)
Includes bibliographical references and index.
Contents: Prologue : who found it? -- Amerigo
Vespucci : leaving his name (1499-1502) -- Pedro
Alvares Cabral : claiming Brazil (1500) -- Juan Dâiaz
de Solâis : on the River of Silver (1516) -- Ferdinand
Magellan : first round the world (1519-21) --
Francisco Pizzaro : builder of Peru, destroyer of the
Incas (1523-41) -- Pedro de Mendoza : the colony of
Buenos Aires (1535-36) -- Francisco de Orellana : on
the Amazon (1541) -- Francis Drake : second round
the world (1577-80) -- Epilogue : what did they find?
-- Important dates on the exploration of South
America.
  ISBN 0-7398-4953-0 (library binding-hardcover) --
ISBN 1-4109-0335-4 (pbk.)
 1. South America--Discovery and exploration--
Juvenile literature. 2. Explorers--South America--
History--Juvenile literature. [1. South America--
Discovery and exploration. 2. Explorers.] I. Naden,
Corinne J. II. Title. III. Series: Blue, Rose.
Exploring the Americas.
  F2233.B58 2004
  980'.013'0922--dc21
                              2003006009

Acknowledgments
The author and publishers are grateful to the
following for permission to reproduce copyright
material:

Cover photographs by Bettmann/Corbis, (map)

Corbis; p. 4 Stapleton Collection/Corbis; pp. 6, 9, 18,
27, 30, 32, 40, 41, 51, 57 Hulton Archive/Getty
Images; pp. 8, 10, 17, 22 Corbis; pp. 12, 37, 55 Mary
Evans Picture Library; p. 14 The Pierpont Morgan
Library/Art Resource, NY; p. 15 Paul Almasy/Corbis;
p. 23 Erich Lessing/Art Resource, NY; p. 24 Jack
Fields/Corbis; p. 25 Konrad Wothe/Minden Pictures;
pp. 34, 39, 54 North Wind Picture Archive; pp. 42,
46 The Granger Collection, New York; p. 45 Pablo
Corral V/Corbis; pp. 47, 49 Wolfgang Kaehler/Corbis;
p. 50 Yann Arthus-Bertrand/Corbis

Photo research by Kathy Creech

Some words are shown in bold,
like **this.** You can find out what
they mean by looking in the glossary.

Contents

Prologue:
Who Found It?

What were they looking for? Before England and France began claiming land in what became North America, Spain looked to the south. Columbus had started the journey west with his first voyage in 1492. Soon Europe began to realize that there was a huge land between it and the Far East.

Columbus and the explorers who followed him did not discover the so-called New World, although it is said they did. North and South America were inhabited long before the Europeans arrived. However, these early explorers recorded what they saw and paved the way for other Europeans to settle in the Americas. They kept journals and drew maps. When these explorers returned home, they brought eyewitness proof that other lands did exist.

After Columbus opened the gates, the exploration rush was on. Spain, always keeping an eye on its archrival, England, was determined to stake its claim to the south. But it soon ran into trouble with another rival, Portugal, which wanted its own New World empire. In 1494 Spain and Portugal signed a treaty that set up an imaginary line in the New World. Everything west of the line went to Spain, everything east went to Portugal. Not surprisingly, other European countries saw no reason to honor this bargain. The result was constant warfare

A 16th-century map shows how Europeans of the time viewed South America.

over European colonies in North and South America.

This is the story of explorers who helped to open the continent of South America to Europe. Five sailed for Spain, one for Portugal, one sailed for Spain and Portugal, and one sailed for England.

Amerigo Vespucci, who gave his name to the Americas, was an Italian in the service of Spain. He also sailed for Portugal. His voyages to South America convinced him that he had not reached Asia but a land previously unknown to Europeans.

Juan de Solis, Ferdinand Magellan, Francisco Pizarro, Pedro de Mendoza, and Francisco de Orellana also sailed

for Spain. Solis was the first European to see the Rio de la Plata. Magellan was born in Portugal and actually sailed for his native land until his voyage for Spain in 1519. This expedition accomplished the first around-the-world voyage. Magellan sailed around South America, through the **strait** now named for him, and out to the Pacific. Pizarro became known for his daring and ruthless methods of conquest. He was a conquistador, which in Spanish means "conqueror." This was a word especially applied to Spain's explorers of the 1400s and 1500s. They gained a reputation for brutality in their conquest of native peoples in the New World. Pizarro overthrew the great civilization of the Incas and founded the city of Lima, Peru, in the first half of the 1500s. Mendoza, a soldier and explorer, founded Buenos Aires, the capital city of modern Argentina, in 1536. He was the first governor of the Rio de la Plata region surrounding it. Orellana was the first to descend the Amazon River.

Pedro Alvares Cabral sailed in the service of Portugal. Sent out to explore new ocean routes for trade between Europe and Asia, he ventured farther west. In 1500 he sighted land that would eventually become the country of Brazil. Earlier explorers had already done so, but Cabral claimed that he actually set foot on the land and took it for Portugal. So he gets the credit.

Francis Drake was the most renowned seaman of England's Elizabethan Age. With the backing of Elizabeth I, he set sail on what would become the second successful voyage around the world. Like Magellan, Drake sailed around the coast of South America heading for the Pacific. His two-year journey, which ended in 1580, made Drake the first captain to sail his own ship around the world. Magellan had died on his voyage around the world; his ship was brought safely home without him.

The story of exploring South America is filled with danger at sea and on land. It tells of the splendor of the Inca Empire and of the fight for gold and other riches. It also tells what happens when different cultures meet and one is determined to conquer the other. Native populations suffered greatly as a result of the European rush for colonization.

The early explorers were reckless, bold, often brutal adventurers who faced the unknown and carried out their missions at whatever the cost. It is from these first voyages to and explorations of South America that the history of the southern continent in the New World is written.

Chapter One

Amerigo Vespucci
Leaving His Name (1499–1502)

Amerigo Vespucci is best known as the man for whom the continents of North and South America are named. But he really earned his place in history for two other reasons. He was the first to realize that the so-called New World was not part of Asia but was a separate, previously unknown continent. He was the first to calculate a nearly correct estimate of the earth's **circumference.** These two events drastically changed the study of geography and mapmaking and earned Vespucci a reputation as one of the world's great explorers.

There is still some dispute over the number of voyages Vespucci made to the Americas. According to some records, Vespucci claimed that he made four voyages to the New World: in 1497, 1499, 1501, and 1503. Most historians, however, believe that he made only two expeditions: in 1499 and 1501.

A child of Florence

Amerigo Vespucci was born in Florence, Italy, in 1451. His education was supervised by his uncle Giorgio Antonio Vespucci, a noted Dominican priest. One of the great orders of the Catholic Church, the Dominicans was founded in 1215. In 1479 the young man accompanied another relative who was sent by the Medicis, a powerful ruling

A portrait depicts Amerigo Vespucci (1451–1512).

family, as their spokesman to the king of France. When Vespucci returned to Florence, he managed a trading firm for the Medicis and was on friendly terms with this famous Italian family.

In 1491 Vespucci was sent by the Medicis to Seville, Spain. There he joined a company, directed by Giannotto Berardi, that fitted ships sailing out of the port city on voyages of discovery. When Berardi died in 1495 or 1496, Vespucci became the manager. It is

thought that he outfitted the first voyage, and possibly the second, of Columbus to the New World. When Columbus returned from his second voyage in 1496, the two men undoubtedly met. There is evidence that even then Vespucci doubted Columbus's claims that he had reached Asia.

The first voyage

According to most historians, by 1499 Vespucci was able to interest the Spanish court in financing his own voyage of discovery. He sailed from Cadiz, Spain, on May 18 with four ships. The voyage was commanded by Alonso de Ojeda, who had sailed on the second expedition with Columbus. Vespucci sailed either as navigator or as the representative of those who backed the voyage.

After a speedy 24-day crossing of the Atlantic, the small fleet reached the northern coast of South America off what is now Guyana. At that point, Ojeda and Vespucci seem to have split up. Ojeda sailed to Hispaniola and Vespucci ventured south. He was the first European to sight the coast of Brazil, on June 27, 1499. He is also credited with being the first to sail into the mouth of the Amazon River, the second longest

waterway in the world. Traveling even further south, he probably reached a point below the present-day city of Recife on the coast of Brazil.

Then Vespucci turned north again, still hugging the coastline. He reached Trinidad, passed the mouth of the

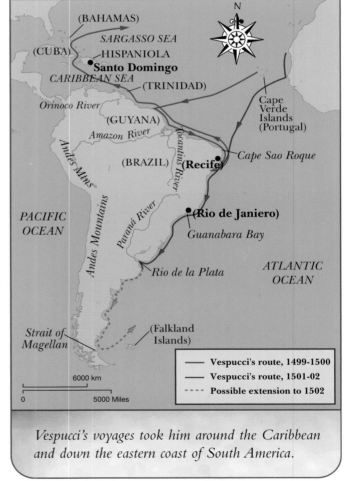

Vespucci's voyages took him around the Caribbean and down the eastern coast of South America.

Orinoco River in Venezuela, and headed for Hispaniola. He stopped at the Spanish colony of Santo Domingo for more supplies and then at the Bahamas, where he kidnapped about 200 Native Americans to be taken back to Spain as slaves. Vespucci returned to Cadiz in June 1500.

When Vespucci had sighted the coast of Brazil, he was convinced that it was Asia, as Columbus and other earlier explorers believed. He thought he was sailing along the extreme easterly **peninsula** of that continent. He thought that ships that passed that point would enter the seas of southern Asia.

A new continent

Vespucci was anxious to prove these theories with a second expedition. However, the Spanish king was not impressed with Vespucci's plans

Today, Rio de Janeiro is the capital of Brazil.

and refused to endorse the voyage. So Vespucci turned to Portugal, which granted approval.

Now sailing in the service of Portugal, Vespucci set out on May 13, 1501, from the port of Lisbon. On the high seas, he apparently passed the ships of explorer Pedro Cabral, who was returning from a voyage to Brazil and India. After a stop at the **Cape** Verde Islands, Vespucci sailed southwestward until he reached the eastern tip of Brazil once again. He hugged the coast and sailed south before entering the harbor of Rio de Janeiro, and sailed as far as the Rio de la Plata between Uruguay and Argentina. Vespucci became the first European to see that river. He may have sailed even farther south, but the details are unknown. He arrived back in Lisbon on July 22, 1502.

Lending his name

The true importance of this second voyage of Amerigo Vespucci was that he returned home with a revolutionary idea. He was now convinced that he had seen not Asia but a previously unknown continent. He was gradually able to convince others as well.

Vespucci returned to the service of Spain, becoming a naturalized citizen in 1505. From 1508 until his death in 1512, he was pilot major of the Spanish kingdom. In this post he helped others prepare for expeditions and compiled all knowledge gained from these voyages. Vespucci himself claimed to have taken

one last voyage in 1503–1504 for the Portuguese government, but this is disputed. In any case no new knowledge resulted from such an undertaking.

Disputed claims and other assertions that cannot be proven or seem implausible in Vespucci's journals have tended to give him a dubious reputation with some scholars. They think perhaps he was trying to steal some of the glory from Columbus. Yet enough is known of his journeys there to honor him as an explorer of importance.

Giving his name to the continents was actually more a mistake than a recognition of his achievements. In 1507 Martin Waldseemuller, a German cartographer, suggested that the newly found lands be named "ab Americo Inventore," or "from Amerigo the discoverer."

In a large drawing belonging to Waldseemuller, the name "America" appears for the first time but is applied only to South America. Applying the name to the northern continent caught on later. It is thought that Waldseemuller believed the account of Vespucci's four voyages, which might have put him on South American soil before Columbus. However it came to be, the New World lands took the name of the first European to realize they were not the continent of Asia.

Ships anchor in the harbor of Lisbon, Portugal.

Chapter Two
Pedro Alvares Cabral
Claiming Brazil (1500)

The European discovery of the largest country in South America was apparently an accident. Pedro Alvares Cabral (c.1467–1520) was really on his way to India. Some also question whether he was actually the first European there. Vespucci sailed along the Brazilian coast before Cabral. Reportedly, so did Vicente Yanez Pinzon and Diego de Lepe. Some say, however, that Cabral actually stepped on the land and the others did not. In any case Cabral seemed unexcited about what he had found. He spent very little time exploring it since he was anxious to get to India. He also didn't seem to be certain of what he had found, a large land mass or a big island. He named it Terra (land) da Vera Cruz, but also referred to it as Ilha (island) da Vera Cruz.

No matter what the true story is, Cabral is generally regarded as the first European to discover Brazil. Brazilians think so, too. Today they celebrate him as the unquestionable **founder** of their country.

Of the nobility

More often than not, Europe's early explorers were men of little wealth and power who went to sea at a young age to earn their fortune. This was not true of Cabral. He was born in 1467 into a

Pedro Alvares Cabral (c.1467–1520)

family of nobility, the son of Pedro Cabral and Isabel de Gouveia, on the family estate in Belmonte, Portugal. The Cabral family had a long history of service to the Portuguese court, and Pedro was no exception. He served as a **page** to King John II and later enjoyed many privileges bestowed upon him by King Manuel I. These included a personal allowance, a seat on the king's council, and membership in the military Order of Christ.

A voyage off-course

In 1499 Cabral was given an even higher honor by the king. He was selected to lead Portugal's second major expedition to India. Following the route of an earlier voyage by Vasco da Gama in 1497, he was to establish trading posts to strengthen the country's commercial ties with India.

Cabral was named admiral in supreme command of 13 ships and 1,000 men. They left the Tagus River at Lisbon on March 9, 1500. Serving with Cabral was Bartolomeu Dias, the first European to see the southern end of Africa in 1488.

On March 18, Cabral sighted the Canary Islands and then the **Cape** Verde Islands on March 22. He changed to a southwesterly direction to take advantage of the trade winds, later heading east to approach the Cape of Good Hope. However, strong **currents** and wind pushed him westward, so much so that on April 22 he sighted land. But it was not India. What Cabral first saw was Mount Pascal in Brazil, about 200 miles (322 kilometers) south of the modern-day city of Salvador.

Because it was around Easter, Cabral named this new land Terra da Vera Cruz, which means Land of the True Cross. However, the name did not last. As soon as traders streamed into the area, they began cutting the forests of pau-brasil, a tree known for its red dye and used in making furniture. The name Brazil was quickly adopted.

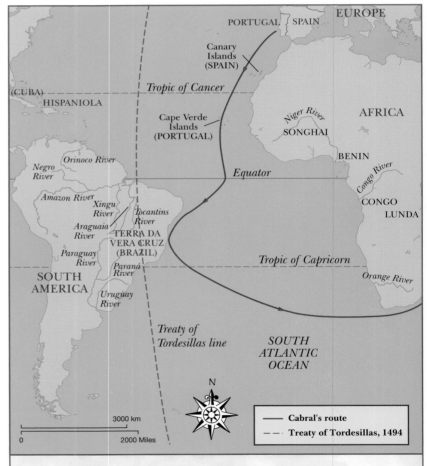

Cabral visited South America before rounding Africa on his way to India.

Cabral stayed in his newly found territory only about ten days, during which he took formal possession for Portugal and, from all records, made an effort to treat the native people with kindness. He explored about 50 miles (80 kilometers) of the coast before leaving. At Porto Seguro (now Baia Cabralia), north of present-day Rio de Janeiro, he planted a cross. Records indicate that Cabral was a democratic leader, which was an oddity for the time. Apparently, he took a vote of the crew on whether to send a ship back to Lisbon with the news of what they had found and whether to send captive Native Americans as well. The crew voted to send the ship but not the Native Americans.

A faded illustration located in the Lisbon Military Museum shows Cabral arriving in Brazil.

Many scholars think Cabral had the Treaty of Tordesillas (1494) in mind when he planted the cross for Portugal. The treaty was aimed at settling conflicts between Spain and Portugal by fixing land boundaries in the Americas. The experts think that Cabral knew just where he was when he landed, knew where the Tordesillas line was, and wanted to make a claim for Portugal before Spain did.

Before long, maps of the region would show Portugal as the ruler of a great expanse of land with vaguely defined boundaries. It became a stopping point for voyagers from Europe to the **Cape** of Good Hope at the tip of Africa, and the Indian Ocean.

On to India

Cabral left Brazil for India and the Cape of Good Hope on May 2, 1500. His good fortune turned to disaster. While rounding the Cape on May 29, four of his ships sank in a storm. All hands were lost. Dias was one of the victims. The remaining ships separated for a while but finally regrouped off the island of Madagascar. They reached Calicut (later known as Calcutta, and today called Kolkata) on the Malabar coast of India on September 13.

The Muslim ruler at Calicut welcomed Cabral and his men and allowed them to set up a fortified trading post there. Before long, however, disputes arose with Muslim traders and on December 17 a large force attacked the fort. About 50 of the Portuguese crew were killed before help could reach them from the ships anchored in the harbor.

Cabral was furious and he retaliated with a vengeance. He bombarded the city, captured ten Muslim ships, and executed their crews. After leaving Calicut, he sailed southward down the Indian coast to the port of Cochin. He received friendly greetings and was allowed to trade. He also established trading posts in the area and negotiated commercial treaties.

On January 16, 1501, Cabral left India for the return trip. His remaining six ships were loaded with precious cargo: spices such as pepper, ginger, cinnamon, and **cloves,** as well as diamonds, black pearls, and porcelain. But disaster struck again. Bad weather sunk two of the vessels. Cabral ended his journey when his four remaining ships reached Portugal on June 23, 1501.

The aftermath

Despite the large loss of life and cargo, King Manuel was very pleased with Cabral's expedition. All the same, when it came time to plan another and bigger voyage to India, it was Vasco da Gama, not Cabral, whom the king chose to lead it. No one knows exactly why Cabral was passed over. Some explanations are that da Gama, who already held the title of admiral of all the fleets, opposed the appointment because he felt that the

This illustration of Cabral's fleet appeared in a 16th-century manuscript.

disasters of Cabral's first expedition should disqualify him for the next.

Pedro Cabral was never again a fixture at the Portuguese court. He retired to an estate near Santarem on the Tagus River, married, and had six children. He died in about 1520 and his tomb at Santarem was identified in 1848 by Brazilian historian Francisco Adolfo Varnhagen. Recognized more in his own time as a trader than as an explorer, Pedro Alvares Cabral is today honored by statues in Lisbon and in Rio de Janeiro, Brazil.

Chapter Three
Juan Diaz de Solis
On the River of Silver (1516)

The Rio de la Plata is a huge arm of the Atlantic Ocean on the southeastern coast of South America between Uruguay and Argentina. The Parana and Uruguay rivers feed into this great **estuary** of freshwater at the river's mouth. Spanish explorer Juan Diaz de Solis (c.1470–1516) made many voyages to the Americas and is said to be the first European to enter this water highway that would be called the river of silver.

Solis spent his early years in Andalusia, Spain.

In the service of Spain

Very little is known about the early life of Solis. He was born in the late 1400s in the small town of Lebrija in the southern Spanish province of Andalusia. Some records say that as a young man he became a sailor in the service of Portugal, making several voyages to India. He may have served for a while with the French military as well. If the story is true, on one expedition he helped to capture a Portuguese **caravel** returning from the Gold Coast. This would have made his return to Portugal impossible, which sent him into the service of Spain by the year 1508.

Now a skilled pilot, Solis apparently made a voyage to the coast of Central America in that year along with Vicente Yanez Pinzon, who had sailed with Columbus in 1492. The small fleet left from the port of Sanlucar de Barrameda, Spain, at the mouth of the Guadalquivir River on June 29, 1508. They were given instructions to find a passage around the Americas. Little is known of their exact route and details are sketchy, but they may have been the first Spanish expedition to reach the

Yucatan **Peninsula** in Mexico. Other reports suggest they spent some time exploring the coast of Veragua (Nicaragua) and attempting to find a passageway to the Spice Islands.

Voyage to South America

Upon his return Solis was apparently looked upon with great favor by King Ferdinand V. So when Amerigo Vespucci died in 1512, leaving the post of pilot major of Spain open, the king appointed Solis to the position. In November 1514 the king commissioned Solis to lead another expedition, this one to an area about 5,000 miles (8,047 kilometers) south of the Isthmus of Panama and beyond. Solis left Sanlucar on October 8, 1515. He led a small fleet of three vessels, 70 men, and provisions for more than two years. His ships were small **caravels** that would allow him to explore shallow coastal waters. His mission was to look for a passage through the Americas to the Pacific.

Solis made a brief stop at the Canary Islands and then set sail southwestward. After working his way down the coast of Brazil in February 1516, he became the first European to enter the mouth of the Rio de la Plata. The **estuary** was so large, Solis named it Mar Dulce, which means "freshwater sea." It was

not given the name of Rio de la Plata until 1527.

Thinking he had found a good passageway to the interior, Solis sailed into the mouth of the river. The first island that he reached he named Martin Garcia, after one of his crewman who had died on the crossing.

After sailing up what is now the Uruguay River, Solis landed on the east bank of modern-day Uruguay. In the heat of August, Solis and some of his men rowed ashore to explore. They were met by the unfriendly Charrua people, who were cannibals. In sight of the crew still on board, Solis and his landing party were attacked, killed, and eaten. Only one crew member,

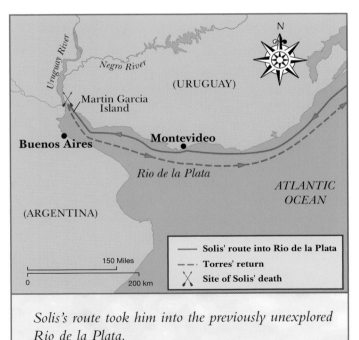

Solis's route took him into the previously unexplored Rio de la Plata.

Francisco del Puerto, was spared and captured. When Sebastian Cabot arrived in the area in 1526, del Puerto was still alive and was able to give the explorer valuable information.

After the massacre the rest of the fleet, now in the command of Solis's brother-in-law, Francisco de Torres, quickly left for Spain. They arrived on September 4, 1516. One of the people who heard their story was Ferdinand Magellan, who would soon have his own tale of adventure.

Some geographers classify the Rio de la Plata as a gulf, while others consider it to be a river.

Chapter Four
Ferdinand Magellan
First Around the World (1519–1521)

A newspaper headline in the year 1521 might have read: "Yes, the Earth Really Is Round." In case there were still doubters, the voyage of Ferdinand Magellan in 1519–1521 returned with proof. Although he died before completing the journey, his was the first voyage to circle the world. He sailed from Spain around the southern tip of South America, through the treacherous waters that would later be called the **Strait** of Magellan, and across the Pacific. After Magellan's death the fleet sailed home around Africa's **Cape** of Good Hope and on to Spain.

Historians rank this achievement as second only to that of Christopher Columbus nearly 30 years earlier. Its success was largely due to Magellan himself: to his skills as a navigator and to his firm, harsh, but fair leadership. He won and kept the respect and loyalty of his crew, without which such a voyage could never have succeeded. Both Columbus and Magellan faced impossible-to-imagine dangers. They had unreliable maps to guide them, crude navigational instruments, and very little knowledge of what might be over the horizon. Once out of sight of land, they were completely on their own. They were at the mercy of weather

A portrait depicts Ferdinand Magellan (c.1480–1521).

or whatever else might arise. In many ways Magellan's journey was even more difficult than that of Columbus: it was longer, went through more treacherous and mysterious seas, and it was larger with a more unruly crew to command. But like Columbus, Magellan opened a new world to the nations of Europe.

An early life at sea

Fernao de Magalhaes (c.1480–1521) is known in history as Ferdinand Magellan,

Portuguese-born navigator and explorer. He was born either in Sabrosa or Ponta de Barca, Portugal, into a family of minor nobility. The youngest of three children, his parents were Donha Alda de Mesquita and Dom Rui de Magalhaes, who was a trusted officer of Portugal's King John II. Magellan was raised in the family home until the age of seven, when he was sent to the monastery school at Vila Nova de Mura. At the age of twelve, he became a **page** in the court of Queen Leonor in Lisbon. There he studied navigation, geography, mathematics, and mapmaking.

King John liked young Magellan, as did the king's successor, Manuel I. When he was fifteen Magellan entered the service of Manuel I. Apparently the king allowed him to go to sea on some of the voyages to advance Portuguese trade. In 1505 Magellan sailed for India in the fleet of Francisco de Almeida, the first Portuguese **viceroy** to the East. The huge expedition of 22 ships and 2,000 men, which was sent to check on Muslim sea power in India and Africa, left Lisbon on March 25.

During a naval engagement at Cannanore on the Malabar Coast of India, Magellan was wounded, one of several wounds he would suffer throughout his career. The Portuguese built a fort at Cannanore and then spent many months patrolling the east African coast. They destroyed Muslim settlements in the area and replaced them with Portuguese

outposts. Details of Magellan's activities are sketchy throughout this period, but in November 1506 he was with Nuno Vaz Pereira in Sofala where they built a fort on the Mozambique coast. Magellan returned to India in 1508 and took part in the Battle of Diu on February 2–3, 1509. He was wounded once again. This fight, in which 200 Muslim ships were destroyed, gave the Portuguese free reign over most of the Indian Ocean.

Attack on Goa

That August Magellan had recovered from his wound and joined Diogo Lopes de Sequeira on a mission to Malacca on the Malay **Peninsula.** Magellan and his cousin, Francisco Serrao, heard news of an impending attack by the Malays against the Portuguese. However, their commanders did not believe the story, and were not ready for an attack when it came. Magellan took part in the fight during which 60 Portuguese were lost.

A few months later, Portuguese ships were attacked by a Chinese pirate ship and Serrao was captured. Magellan boarded the vessel, rescued his cousin, and claimed the loot that was in the hold. Unfortunately, the ship went down in a storm as it was being towed, and the treasure was lost.

In October the new viceroy Afonso de Albuquerque made plans for recapturing the city of Goa, but Magellan advised against it. Nevertheless, the city was

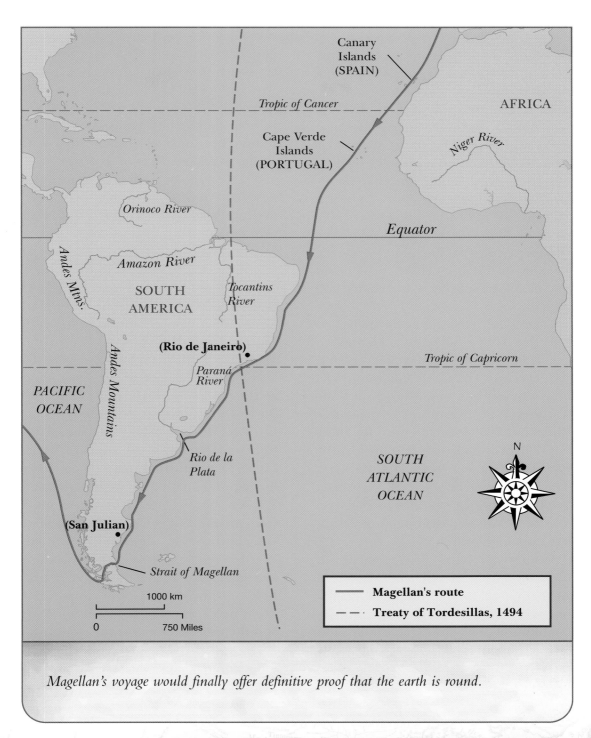

Canary
Islands
(SPAIN)

Tropic of Cancer

AFRICA

Cape Verde
Islands
(PORTUGAL)

Niger River

Orinoco River

Equator

Andes Mtns.

Amazon River

SOUTH
AMERICA

*Tocantins
River*

(Rio de Janeiro)

*Paraná
River*

Tropic of Capricorn

PACIFIC
OCEAN

Andes Mountains

*Rio de la
Plata*

SOUTH
ATLANTIC
OCEAN

N

(San Julian)

Strait of Magellan

1000 km

0   750 Miles

——	**Magellan's route**
- - -	**Treaty of Tordesillas, 1494**

Magellan's voyage would finally offer definitive proof that the earth is round.

subject to a brutal attack by the Portuguese on November 24. Although there was wholesale slaughtering and **pillage,** there is no evidence that Magellan was part of it even though he is believed to have been present. His name does not appear in Albuquerque's account of the battle, nor is he listed as receiving any of the spoils. After the battle, however, Albuquerque promoted him to captain in command of a **caravel.**

By June 1511 Malacca (now Melaka) on the Malay **peninsula** had fallen to the Portuguese. This gave them control of shipping the riches of the East to their home ports in the West. While on this expedition, Magellan came upon a thirteen-year-old Malay boy whom he called Black Henry or Mallaca Henry. The boy remained with Magellan for the rest of the captain's life.

In the service of Spain

Magellan was back in Lisbon in 1512 but stayed only a short time. The following year he went into battle against the Moroccan stronghold of Azemmour. The Portuguese were victorious, but Magellan sustained another wound. This one would leave him with a permanent limp. So in late 1514 Magellan petitioned King Manuel for an increase in his pension. But the king refused, possibly because he had heard a rumor that Magellan had stolen some of the loot captured in the Azemmour battle. The charges were later dropped. Magellan waited two years to petition the king

again. Once again he was refused. Manuel even told the navigator to offer his services elsewhere.

Rebuffed, angry, and insulted, Magellan did as the king suggested. He went to Seville, Spain, arriving on October 20, 1517. In Seville he married Beatriz Barbosa, a daughter of a city official and a relative of Duarte Barbosa, who had served with Magellan during the Indian campaigns. The marriage was prearranged.

With mapmaker and astronomer Rui Faleiro, Magellan journeyed to Valladolid to offer his services to a young King Charles I, who would later become Emperor Charles V. Magellan renounced his Portuguese citizenship and from then on he was known in Spain as Fernando de Magallanes.

The bold proposal

Early in 1518 Magellan and Faleiro presented the king with a bold proposal. A papal **proclamation** in 1493 had drawn an imaginary line concerning the so-called New World territories. The line was redrawn in 1494 in the Treaty of Tordesillas. All claims east of the line belonged to Portugal, and all claims west belonged to Spain. This was supposed to settle the constant warfare over New World territory between the two nations. It mainly served to anger other European countries such as Great Britain. Now Magellan and Faleiro proposed to sail west to prove that the enormously rich Spice Islands (Molluccas) were in the

Spanish zone. Europeans had known about the Spice Islands for centuries. Marco Polo knew roughly where they were in the 1200s. But no one was certain how the line drawn by the Tordesillas treaty affected the other side of the world. If Spain could claim the islands, it would mean fabulous wealth in the form of spices, palm oil, teak, **quinine,** dyes, pepper, and other coveted items. By sailing continuously westward, the explorers would avoid the **Cape** of Good Hope at the tip of Africa, which was controlled by the Portuguese.

Such an idea defied the conventional sailing plans of the time. Magellan's proposal was indeed bold and experimental, but it was not original. Others had proposed sailing westward but had never done it. This time the young king accepted the proposal.

Magellan and Faleiro were appointed joint captains general of the voyage and were directed to find an all-Spanish route to the Molluccas, which lay west of New Guinea. They would receive a one-twentieth share of the profits. The lands they discovered would be given to them and their heirs. The two men were admitted into the Order of Santiago, a religious-military group of knights founded in about 1160 to fight the Spanish Muslims.

Officials readied five ships in Seville for the expedition. All were small or medium-sized sailing vessels. Magellan's **flagship** was the *Trinidad*. The others, with captains appointed by the king,

were the *Concepcion, Victoria, Santiago,* and the *San Antonio.* Largest of the ships, the *San Antonio* was commanded by Juan de Cartagena. He was promoted to second in command to replace Faleiro who was suffering from mental illness. In May King Charles gave Magellan a set of instructions directing how the voyage should be conducted. He specified how records should be kept, how native peoples should be treated (things the people should and should not do), and what was expected to be gained from the venture. In early October 1519 Magellan said

Charles V (1500–1558) ruled Spain as Charles I before becoming Holy Roman Emperor at age 19.

The Victoria *was one of the ships involved in Magellan's around-the-world voyage.*

goodbye to his wife and infant son in Seville and traveled to Sanlucar to begin the first expedition around the world.

Westward, ho!

On September 20, 1519, Ferdinand Magellan began his fantastic voyage. The five ships carried nearly 214,000 pounds (97,069 kilograms) of biscuits and 72,000 pounds (32,659 kilograms) of salt beef plus cheese, rice, figs, onions, knives, fishhooks, trading goods, armament, and supplies for repairs. The crew numbered about 250 men, including Spanish and Portuguese. Magellan himself picked most of the officers and pilots, who were Portuguese. The fact that there were sailors from two rival nations on board caused a good deal of tension as did the fact that no one told the crew where they were going. This was not unusual when a captain felt that such disclosure might prevent him from assembling a crew at all.

The fleet reached Tenerife in the Canary Islands on September 26 and left for Brazil on October 3. Trouble began when the ships turned west from the African coast. Cartagena led a group of rebel sailors who hoped to prod Magellan into an act that would justify killing him. But Magellan acted calmly and firmly. He appointed a new captain of the *San Antonio* and imprisoned Cartagena.

The tension was not eased by the weather. First, the expedition ran into terrible storms. Then the wind died altogether and they waited motionless on the calmed sea. Magellan finally sighted the coast of Brazil on December 8 and entered the Bay of Rio de Janeiro five days later. Calling it Porto de Santa Lucia, Magellan anchored there to repair the ships.

Tenerife in the Canary Islands is located about 60 miles (95 kilometers) from the coast of Africa.

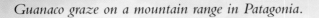

Guanaco graze on a mountain range in Patagonia.

From Santa Lucia Magellan sailed south along the coast looking for a passageway that would lead them around South America and to the East. Magellan thought he had found it in early January 1520 when he reached the wide Rio de la Plata, which he searched in vain. Now he turned south once more, entering waters that only Vespucci might have seen before him.

For two months Magellan searched for a passage. Finally, on March 31, he decided to anchor for the winter at present-day San Julian in southern Argentina. It was there that the men saw strange animal life such as guanaco, which is a kind of llama that looks like a camel. It was also there that Magellan experienced the second crew uprising on Easter day. It was led by Gaspar de

Quesada, one of the Spanish captains, who freed Cartagena and tried to stage a revolt. He promised all who sided with him that they would return safely to Spain at once. However, the majority of the crew stuck with Magellan. With their help he put down the mutiny quickly and firmly. Quesada was tried and executed. Cartagena and a priest who had been part of the mutiny were left in desolate Argentina when the ships sailed away. Magellan was not by nature a harsh or cruel man, but he was convinced that no sea voyage could succeed without strict discipline.

During the months spent at San Julian, repairs were made to the five ships. However, after Magellan sent the *Santiago* south on a scouting trip, the ship ran aground. The crew was saved, but Magellan was down to four ships. Magellan also discovered that he was short on provisions and had only enough to last about three months. The Portuguese merchants who had supplied provisions for the voyage had obviously hoped to ensure its failure because Magellan was sailing for Spain. Magellan, however, had no intention of turning back.

At San Julian Magellan first saw a Native American whom he called Juan Gigante (giant in Spanish) because the man was so big. When he met others like him, he called them patagoes, meaning "big feet" in Portuguese,

because they wore huge guanaco skins for shoes. Today the southern region of Argentina is known as Patagonia.

Before they set sail again, Magellan had more trouble with the crew, this time the remaining captains of the other vessels. They were unhappy over not being consulted whenever Magellan ordered a change in course or time-table. When Magellan removed the captains from their duties, a fight followed and three of them were killed.

The strait

On August 24, 1520, the fleet of four ships with three new captains left San Julian and sailed south. They reached the mouth of the Santa Cruz River. In mid-October, seeing that the coastline was turning east, Magellan sent the San Antonio ahead to explore the region with instructions to return in three days. Instead the captain of the San Antonio sailed the ship back to Spain.

Now reduced to three ships, Magellan rounded the **Cape** of the Virgins (Cabo de las Virgenes). Even though he had no idea where this inlet led, he sent his fleet into the water passage between the Atlantic and Pacific Oceans. This passage now bears his name. It was a long and difficult journey, taking 37 days to complete. Later explorers would make the journey in far less or far greater time depending on weather conditions. But the passage was rarely easy. Magellan separated the ships

A print shows Magellan discovering the path to the Pacific.

so that they could explore the many channels of the **strait** to see which one would lead to the Pacific Ocean and the Far East. The **current** was treacherous. Navigation was tricky as cliffs rose sharply from the sides of the strait and huge **whirlpools** seemed to drag the vessels under. To the south the horizon looked to be on fire and Magellan called it Tierra del Fuego (Land of Fire).

Finally, on November 27, 1520, the *Trinidad, Concepcion,* and *Victoria* sailed out the other side. It is said that Magellan cried when he saw the western ocean and unfurled the flag of Castille for Spain. Because the waters seemed so calm after the stormy sail through the **strait,** Magellan expressed the wish that it always remain as calm and benevolent. "In this hope," he said, "I name it the

Pacific Ocean." He named the **cape** at the most western end Cape Desire.

The perilous time

The difficult sail through the strait was behind them. What lay ahead was far more torturous.

Magellan now began the great crossing of the Pacific. The journey would take five months. After entering the Pacific Magellan sailed north, passing between the coast of Chile and the Juan Fernandez Islands. Then he steered west-northwest. Since he had only crude navigational tools, historians are not certain of his exact route. The voyage to the Moluccas, expected to take about a month, seemed never to end. Food was getting scarce and freshwater supplies were low. The crew tried to catch fish. They had taken seal and penguin meat aboard but, without refrigeration, it rotted in the heat. One by one, the crew began to die from hunger, from thirst, and from a lack of fresh vegetables, which brought on scurvy. Sometimes they were reduced to catching and eating the rats that scurried around the ships.

According to Magellan's calculations, by Christmas they reached 10 degrees South. That is the latitude of the Molluccas. But they saw nothing. In January 1521 a disgusted Magellan threw his maps into the sea. Just a few days later they saw land. It was probably the uninhabited island of Pukapuka in the Tuamotu Archipelago. Magellan called it St. Paul in honor of the patron saint. The ships anchored to catch rainfall and fill the **casks.** After about a week, they continued on their west-northwest course, crossing the equator on February 13.

Tragedy in the Philippines

On March 6 the weary fleet reached the island of Guam in the Ladrones, now called the Marianas. For the first time in more than three months, the voyagers tasted fresh food. The men went ashore to gather coconuts and rice.

Three days later, Magellan steered a west-southwestward course. By March 16 he reached Samar in a group of islands he called the Archipelago de San Lazaro, named after Saint Lazarus. They would later be renamed the Philippines for King Philip II of Spain. The ships anchored off present-day Humuno and were met by native islanders who, although they appeared to have few possessions, wore bracelets and trinkets made of gold.

The sight of gold caused a change in Magellan's plans. Although the crew was anxious to move on to the Molluccas, Magellan decided to stay for a while. He sailed the fleet to the island of Massava (Limasawa) on March 28. The native peoples appeared to accept them. In fact their leader, Colambu, joined the officers and men when they celebrated mass on Easter.

Magellan had several reasons for spending time on Massava. As with all the early explorers, the lure of gold was

powerful. Additional islands might be discovered in the archipelago, and the king had promised Magellan that he could keep any group of six or more that he discovered. Magellan wanted to find a **landmark** that would verify what he already knew; that he had encircled the globe. When they landed on Massava, a Native American spoke to Magellan's servant, Henry, in Henry's own Malay language. Magellan, who had earlier sailed in the Indies, recognized that he had completed the circle.

In addition to those reasons, Magellan thought that the native peoples might be converted to Christianity. No matter how they treated native peoples or the number of men they killed in battle, most of the men who sailed for Spain were devoutly religious. It was their duty to convert what they thought of as **heathens** to Christianity.

Chief Colambu seemed amiable to the idea of conversion and took Magellan to meet another leader on the nearby island of Cebu. By mid-April, the Spanish had built a stone chapel on the island and celebrated mass. The next step was to baptize both chiefs.

Now the same stubbornness and firmness of character that had served Magellan so well on the high seas would bring about his death. He also ignored one of the firm instructions of the king on the treatment of native peoples. Not content with his progress on Cebu, Magellan ordered all the other native leaders in the area to become Christians.

The first one to refuse saw his village burned. When the chief of the Mactan refused, Magellan decided to set an example. Against the advice of his officers and the Cebu chief, he sailed to the island of Mactan with 60 of his men and attacked the village.

As the Spaniards began to burn the Mactan houses, they were attacked by about 1,000 warriors armed with stones and arrows. The battle raged the entire day of April 27, 1521. When it became clear that even the Spanish muskets and crossbows could not stop the onslaught, Magellan ordered his men to retreat. But it was too late. First an arrow pierced his leg and then his arm. When he was wounded for a third time, the explorer fell to the ground and died.

The journey home

With their captain dead, the rest of the crew fled from Mactan and returned to Cebu where Juan Serrano and Duarte Barbosa assumed command. However, they also ignored the instructions of the king. They accepted an invitation from the Cebu chief to attend a banquet with about 30 of the crew. At the banquet, they were all killed by the native islanders.

Now with a much smaller crew, the decision was made to burn the *Concepcion* and continue with two ships. Gonzalo Gomez de Espinosa was elected captain general of the Trinidad and Juan Sebastian del Cano commanded the *Victoria*. Del Cano was the original commander of the *Concepcion*. He had

Magellan was killed in a battle against the Mactan people.

until they reached Tidore in the Moluccas. The expedition had taken more than two years to get to this intended site. Greeted warmly by Sultan Almanzor, the Spaniards loaded the ships with **cloves,** a highly valued spice.

When the ships left the Moluccas, the *Trinidad* was weighed down and badly in need of repair. It was decided that Espinosa would turn back for repairs and del Cano would continue the journey with the records of the voyage.

Del Cano headed for the island of Timor, then crossed the Indian Ocean far to the south to keep out of reach of any Portuguese ships that commanded the area. He sighted the **Cape** Verde Islands on July 13, 1522. At this point, Del Cano became the first person to discover a fact not yet known to any sailor of the seas. All the records of the voyage were off by one day. This is because in traveling east to west, which is opposite to the rotation of the earth, the traveler "loses" one day. The explanation for this phenomenon is that a traveler going east to west is traveling "against" the sun. Each sun-

participated in the Port San Julian mutiny, but somehow escaped punishment by Magellan.

The ships left Cebu and sailed through the Philippines with stops at Mindanao and several smaller islands

rise to sunset is slightly longer than 24 hours because of the distance traveled. That accumulated difference totals exactly one day when going completely around the globe. Today this difference is adjusted by establishing the so-called International Date Line, the imaginary line extending between the North and South Poles along 180 degrees longitude to mark off one day from the next.

On September 8, 1522, the last remaining ship of the first voyage around the world returned to Spain. On board were del Cano, 17 of the original 250-man crew, and four East Indians. Fortunately one of the survivors was a sailor named Pigafetta, who kept a record of the nearly three-year (only short by 14 days) voyage. It is through his shared and complete journal that the rest of the world learned the details of Magellan's incredible journey. The journal was published in 1523. In it Pigafetta called Magellan "so noble a captain."

Del Cano and the survivors were received with great honor and joy as news traveled quickly about the fantastic feat. The treasure of **cloves** was sold for an excellent price, and the survivors were given some of the profits. Emperor Charles V presented del Cano with an addition to his coat of arms. It was a globe with the inscription "The First One to Circle Me." Magellan would receive history's honors, but del Cano was the first to bring back practical proof that the earth indeed was round.

As for Espinosa, left behind by chance on the damaged *Trinidad,* he returned to Tidore only to find that the Portuguese had attacked and captured the island. Espinosa was also captured and kept a prisoner until 1526. When he was released, he made his way back to Spain alone and by land.

Tribute to Magellan

Although Ferdinand Magellan never lived to see its completion, his journey was a nearly unbelievable accomplishment in that time. A man of complex character, he possessed the bold vision to face the unknown and the fierce will to hold together a small, unruly band who never realized their journey would change the world.

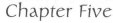

Chapter Five
Francisco Pizarro
Builder of Peru, Destroyer of the Incas (1523–1541)

Hailed as one of Spain's greatest conquistadors, Francisco Pizarro was a clever and ruthless leader who conquered the Inca Empire, brought the land of Peru directly under Spanish control, and changed the future of South America. His brutal conquests made Spain the major European power of its time.

The early years

Francisco Pizarro (c.1475–1541) never learned to read. He was born in Trujillo in the province of Estremadura, Spain. His father, Gonzalo Pizarro, was an army captain. His mother, Francisca Gonzalez, was a young peasant woman. He grew up in his mother's home but was accepted into his father's family as well. Little is known of his early years except that he had no formal education at all and probably worked herding pigs, as did many boys in the region.

Pizarro likely fought in local wars among landlords and, as a soldier of fortune, drifted off to fight in Italy as well. It is known that in 1502, when he was about 27 years old, he sailed to Hispaniola (modern-day Haiti and Dominican Republic) in the fleet of Nicolas de Ovando, the new governor.

Francisco Pizarro (c.1475–1541)

The explorer

Pizarro apparently had no taste for colonial life, so in 1510 he joined Alonso de Ojeda on his expedition to the Gulf of Uraba in present-day Colombia. He seems to have been a silent, not overly ambitious man who could be trusted with difficult problems. Pizarro helped to establish a settlement and was left in charge when Ojeda departed to obtain

needed supplies. In 1513 he was promoted to captain and joined the expedition of Vasco Nuñez de Balboa across Darien in Panama. Balboa is credited as the first European to see the Pacific Ocean. Pizarro may well have been the second.

During this expedition Pizarro first heard tales of a kingdom that was the home of the Inca Empire. He never forgot the stories of gold in the region. For the next few years, from 1519 until 1523, Pizarro served as mayor of the newly established town of Panama. He also became a cattle breeder and trader and accumulated a small fortune.

Earning a reputation

In 1523, when he was about 48 years old, Pizarro began the adventure that would bring him lasting fame. In partnership with a soldier named Diego de Almagro and a priest named Hernando de Luque, he petitioned the governor of Panama, Pedro Arias de Avila (called Pedrarias). Pizarro wanted to launch a voyage of discovery and conquest down the western coast of South America. He would search for the civilization of riches reported to exist there.

Permission was granted. Luque supplied the funds, and Pizarro and Almagro sailed from Panama in November 1524. They explored the

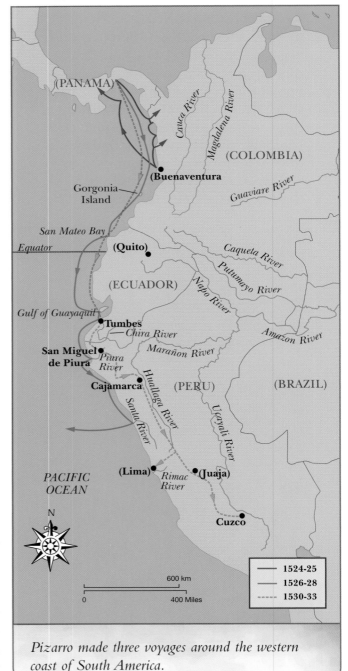

Pizarro made three voyages around the western coast of South America.

Pacific coast of modern-day Colombia as far south as Buenaventura. However, the entire expedition suffered greatly from disease, starvation, and Native American attacks. Pizarro pushed on until the loss of two-thirds of his 80-man crew forced him to return to Panama. It was an early and disappointing end, especially since he had not found even a trace of a wealthy civilization.

There was even more disturbing news back in Panama. Most of the crew that survived the expedition refused to sail with him again. They called Pizarro a fanatic and a killer.

However, in 1526 a second expedition was readied with Luque once more supplying the funds. Getting money for the voyage was easy compared to getting a crew to sign up for it. Most of the sailors had heard the story of the first expedition. In the end, however, the lure of possible riches convinced 160 men to agree to the journey. Pizarro and

Pizarro draws a line in the sand, inspiring a number of men to defy orders and follow Pizarro to Peru.

Almagro left Panama on March 10 in two ships to search along the Colombian coast. When they did find some traces of gold, Pizarro sent the pilot Bartolome Ruiz to explore farther south. Ruiz crossed the equator and returned with stories of a land rich in gold and silver. He is said to be the first European to see what became the country of Peru.

Now the whole expedition sailed south to the community of Tumbes on the Bay of Guayaquil in Ecuador. The newcomers were met by Native Americans who greeted them in boats made of balsa wood and gave them exotic foods. Although Tumbes did not represent the actual splendor of the Inca Empire, Pizarro saw indications of an advanced civilization and heard tales of gold and great wealth.

Feeling that he did not have enough men for a conquest of the region, Pizarro sent Almagro back to Panama for reinforcements. Instead of aid the new governor at Darien ordered Pizarro and his men to return. He wanted no more lives lost in the attempt to find this mythical empire.

According to legend, when Pizarro heard the governor's reply he is said to have drawn a line in the sand with his sword. With this defiance of orders, he changed the fate of a continent. Speaking to his crew, he pointed north to indicate Panama and a life of peace and poverty. Pointing south to Peru, he indicated a chance for wealth and glory for those who dared to cross the line.

Reportedly, just thirteen of Pizarro's men crossed the line.

Pizarro took the thirteen men south to below the equator and into the land he called Peru. The name was probably a corruption of Viru, a name of a river. During three separate landings along the coast, he discovered evidence of gold and artifacts indicating a highly developed civilization. He also heard stories of a rich empire in the interior led by a rich and powerful king.

Pizarro returned to Panama convinced that he now had evidence to justify a voyage of conquest. But the governor still opposed the venture. So Pizarro decided to sail to Spain to ask permission of Emperor Charles V. He left Panama in the spring of 1528, arriving in Seville at the same time as Hernan Cortes, who had just conquered Mexico. That achievement apparently helped to put the king in a good mood. When Pizarro appeared before the royal court in July 1529, he was given a coat of arms and made captain general of the province of New Castile for some 600 miles (966 kilometers) south of Panama along the coast. Almagro and Luque were somewhat dismayed to get lesser compensations. Given all the rights and authority of a **viceroy,** Pizarro was authorized to conquer the vast area that today includes Ecuador, Bolivia, Peru, and northern Chile.

In January 1530 Pizarro returned to Panama along with his half-brothers Gonzalo, Hernando, Juan, and Martin,

and a group of recruits. But it was not until the following January that he was ready for the expedition to Peru. He set sail in one ship with 180 men and 37 horses. Two ships would follow.

The voyage to Tumbes was delayed by bad weather, but when they finally arrived they found the city in ruins. The devastation was partly the result of a civil war within the Inca Empire and partly due to the act that the earlier visit by the Spaniards had left the villagers with the dreaded disease **smallpox,** from which many died or became seriously ill.

Pizarro took the city of Tumbes without opposition. Soon after, Sebastian de Benalcazar arrived by ship with 30 men, followed by Hernando de Soto before his trip to what is now the southeastern United States. He supplied horses and 100 more soldiers. In May 1532 Pizarro explored the Chira River and northwestern Peru, where he founded the town of San Miguel de Piura. Leaving behind 60 of his men to hold the settlement, Pizarro left with 62 men on horseback and 106 foot soldiers. He led his small army through very difficult mountain terrain to reach his goal. He was ready to realize his dream of conquering the empire of the Incas.

Empire of the Incas

Pizarro was bent on conquering a civilization that in 1530 was at the height of its splendor. It stretched along the Pacific Coast from Ecuador to central Chile, controlling a population of about 12 million people. The Inca Empire had founded its capital at Cuzco (interior southeastern Peru) in the 1100s and had begun conquests of the region three centuries later.

The Incas left no written records, so their history is known only through oral tradition. The **founder** of the **dynasty** was Manco Capac, but it was not until the fourth emperor, Mayta Capac, in the 1500s, that they began to expand into surrounding territories. After a region was conquered, a number of the defeated people were transferred to another area. This ensured political and ethnic stability throughout the empire. Local governors collected a tax on labor, which paid for the empire's expenses. The tax could also be paid by serving in the army or doing public works.

Incan society was very rigid. The emperor at the top exercised supreme authority and often used harsh controls. Agriculture was highly developed and was the basis of the economy. Almost every Incan man was a farmer, growing maize (corn), squash, tomatoes, coca, potatoes, peanuts, and cotton. People lived in stone or **adobe** huts. Irrigation systems were highly developed, as was Incan architecture, evident in palaces and temples throughout the region.

Ironically, one of the best features of the Incan society helped to defeat them so quickly. The empire had an enormous complex of roads. Two main roads ran north and south for more

The last emperor of the Incas, Atahualpa, is carried on a litter to meet Pizarro.

than 2,000 miles (3,219 kilometers) each with an array of connecting links. The system was mainly used for the military, and it eased the movement of Pizarro and his forces when they arrived.

Religion in the empire included the sacrifice of animals and humans and a worship of nature gods, headed by the sun god, Inti. The Spanish destroyed most of the religious temples and palaces when they conquered the empire.

Today's descendants of the Inca make up about 45 percent of Peru's population. They are Quechua-speaking peasants who are generally farmers and herders. Their religion is Roman Catholic blended with the veneration of ancient spirits and gods.

Conquest of the Inca

When Pizarro undertook the mission to conquer the Incas, the empire had recently been through internal strife. Around 1527 Chief Huayna-Capac and his heir had died of an epidemic, probably smallpox. Two of the emperor's sons took

charge. Huascar ruled the city of Cuzco and Atahualpa governed Quito. In a civil war that followed, Atahualpa defeated his brother and took over the kingdom.

By April of 1530, Pizarro had made contact with Atahualpa, who was encamped in the city of Cajamarca. In mid-November Pizarro sent his brother Hernando to request an interview. Atahualpa accepted and was carried into the city square on a litter escorted by about 3,000 of his men, who were either unarmed or carried short clubs and slings beneath their tunics. The Incan leader actually had a much larger force in the hills outside the city.

Through a priest, Pizarro asked Atahualpa to accept Christianity as his religion and Charles V as his master. Atahualpa declined, throwing the Bible that was given to him to the ground.

Pizarro immediately ordered an attack and the astonished Incas were cut down from all sides by the onslaught. In the confusion that followed the Spaniards slashed with their swords and bodies began to pile in the square. The defeat was overwhelming, accomplished with fewer than 200 Spanish soldiers. In the battle, Pizarro himself seized the chief and took him captive.

To secure his release, Altahualpa offered to give Pizarro a room filled with gold and silver. In modern terms the treasure is thought to have been worth about $100 million. Eventually the ransom was gathered and delivered

as promised. Instead of being released, Altahualpa was charged by Pizarro with murdering his brother, Huascar, and of plotting to overthrow the Spaniards. The chief of the Incas was ordered to be burned to death, over the objections of Hernando Pizarro and de Soto. Pizarro compromised only slightly. Altahualpa was put to death by strangulation on August 29, 1533.

When they heard of their leader's death, the surrounding Incan armies retreated. Pizarro and his men began the march toward the capital city of Cuzco. The passage through the Andes was made possible by the Incas themselves and their fine network of roads. Pizarro and his troops marched more than 750 miles (1,207 kilometers) through mountain ranges in the cold, thin air of the higher altitudes. Along the way, they fought four battles, but the Native Americans were no match for the Spanish, most of them on horseback, and their armor.

Pizarro entered the royal city of Cuzco on November 15, 1533, without a struggle. The mighty Inca Empire had fallen. Pizarro had conquered Peru.

The conquest was not quite complete, however. He set up a puppet ruler for all of Peru in the person of Atahualpa's brother Manco. On January 10, 1535, he founded a new capital city at the coast on the Rimac River, calling it La Ciudad de Los Reyes (City of Kings). Later, it became Lima and remains the capital of Peru.

Die by the sword

Francisco Pizarro was true to his oath. He conquered the Inca Empire and the land of Peru. But he spent the rest of his life defending his territory and his wealth from other conquistadors. To keep them busy elsewhere, he often sent conquistadors on expeditions to present-day Chile, Colombia, and Ecuador. And for all his success as a warrior, he was a poor administrator. He remained basically unschooled and had no experience working in government. In fact, he did not take an active role in governing his land. The Inca's system of agriculture and irrigation fell into ruin. Torture and assault were commonplace, and the native peoples were enslaved.

Even worse for Pizarro, trouble developed between him and his old friend Almagro, mostly over the unlimited powers given to Pizarro by the king. At one point Almagro even seized the city of Cuzco but was persuaded

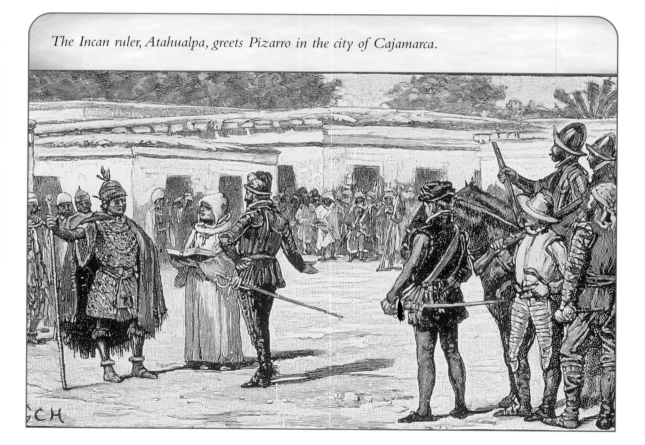

The Incan ruler, Atahualpa, greets Pizarro in the city of Cajamarca.

Pizarro is attacked and killed while at dinner.

city, Almagro was killed by Hernando Pizarro in the Battle of Las Salinas in April 1538. This potential civil war did not go unnoticed in Spain, and Hernando was ordered back to Madrid where he was imprisoned for Almagro's murder. He stayed in prison until 1561.

Meanwhile, in Peru followers of Almagro united behind his son Francisco. Suspecting that Pizarro would eventually try to get rid of them, they decided to attack first. On June 26, 1541, the Almagro backers broke into Pizarro's palace as he was entertaining guests at dinner. Although he defended himself, he was brought down by multiple stab wounds. As Pizarro felt to the ground, he is said to have drawn a cross in his own blood and said the word "Jesus." So it was that the ruthless man who lived by the sword also died by the sword.

Pizarro is buried in the presidential palace in Lima, Peru. In 1977 archaeologist Hugo Ludena found his coffin with a separate lead box that contained the conquistador's head.

instead to go to Chile, where the king had granted Pizarro extensive powers. But Almagro was dismayed at the poverty there and returned in 1537 when he helped to put down a revolt in Lima. However, when he tried to take over the

Francisco Pizarro conquered the kingdoms of Peru and brought vast territory and wealth to his native country. He made Spain the major power of its time. He amassed an enormous fortune for himself. As was the

Three young girls in Cuzco walk beside a wall that dates back to Incan times.

custom with almost all Spanish explorers, he established Catholicism as the religion of the land he conquered. But for all his skills as an explorer, for all his bravery in facing the unknown, Pizarro is most of all remembered as a ruthless warrior who brutally conquered a native people. In doing so he helped to shape the future of the New World's southern continent.

Chapter Six
Pedro de Mendoza
The Colony of Buenos Aires (1535–1536)

The capital city of Buenos Aires, Argentina, is a sprawling metropolis and port on the Rio de la Plata, 150 miles (241 kilometers) from the Atlantic Ocean. A center of government and culture with a population of 13.5 million, it began as a troubled settlement in the early 1500s. The **founder** was Pedro de Mendoza, a Spanish soldier and explorer who spent one year in his new colony and died on the voyage back to Spain. Oddly enough, although he is credited as the founder of Buenos Aires, the original colony failed and a second settlement attributed to his expedition in modern-day Paraguay was successful.

In the king's service

Pedro de Mendoza (1487–1537) was born in Guadix, Granada, Spain. Little is known of his childhood except that his family was distinguished. As a young man he was an officer in the military during Spanish campaigns in Italy.

When Emperor Charles V (Charles I of Spain) became excited by the reports of great wealth found in the Inca Empire conquered by Pizarro, he was determined to make sure that Spain was the first nation to explore the interior of the southern continent. The king made plans to colonize the Rio de la Plata area on its western coast. He appointed

A drawing depicts Pedro de Mendoza (1487–1537).

Mendoza to head the expedition, giving him the title of adelantado. Mendoza was authorized to found three cities and to claim Spanish domination over an extensive region, establishing himself as the ruler for the rest of his life. As was usual in deals of this kind, Mendoza was promised a generous share of any treasures that he discovered.

To South America

The expedition was financed by loans from Flemish and Dutch bankers made to Charles V. It was a relatively large and

well-organized undertaking. Mendoza sailed on August 24, 1535, with thirteen ships and about 2,000 men. That was more than three times the number who had accompanied Cortes when he conquered Mexico about sixteen years earlier. Two more ships were added when the fleet stopped at the Canary Islands.

But the voyage had bad luck from the start. Most importantly, Mendoza himself was ill, suffering from syphilis. This disease could go undetected for years, but it could also cause serious problems—such as blindness—and was often fatal. (There was little treatment at the time, but since the 1940s syphilis can be effectively treated with penicillin.) The weather was so bad that two ships were forced to turn back and the rest of the fleet became separated. Some managed to reach the Rio de la Plata area. Others, including Mendoza's ship, dropped anchor at Rio de Janeiro, where they stayed for two weeks because Mendoza was ill. During this period Juan Osorio was given command. Mendoza then accused him of mutiny and, although there was no positive proof, had Osorio executed.

Finally, the entire expedition was assembled in the Rio de la Plata in early 1536. Mendoza

founded a settlement that he called Santa Maria del Buen Aire (Saint Mary of the Good Air) after a mariner's shrine in the port of Sanlucar, Spain. The size of the fleet now proved a handicap. Food became a major problem. It was the end of the summer in the southern hemisphere and it was impossible to plant seeds to grow food. The **estuary** provided fish but not enough to sustain so many men. At first the neighboring

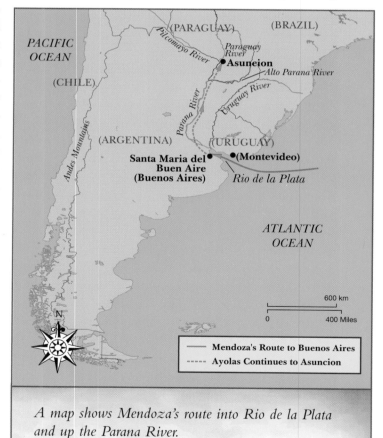

A map shows Mendoza's route into Rio de la Plata and up the Parana River.

native people were helpful in supplying food, but they soon grew tired of the impossible task and disappeared into the wilderness.

The lack of food caused the Spaniards to slaughter not only their cattle but their horses as well. Some even resorted to cannibalism. In this weakened condition the Spaniards were no match for a band of Native Americans who laid siege to the camp in June 1536. Mendoza lost 26 men including his brother, Diego. This attack was followed by constant harassment from the Querandi and other native peoples in the region.

The second settlement

While waiting for assistance from Spain, Mendoza sent his deputy, Pedro de Ayolas, north to search for the fabled Native American kingdom in the interior. Ayolas took about 400 men and set off along the Parana River. The journey took two months. Sometimes they met friendly Native Americans, and sometimes they traveled for days without seeing another human.

After the expedition left the Parana and traveled into modern-day Paraguay in the interior of South America, they met the Carios people. The Carios lived along the Rio Paraguay near where it joins the Pilcomayo. A German soldier named Huldrich Schmidt had accompanied the expedition and kept records of the journey. According to Schmidt, Ayolas was particularly disgusted with the Carios because they ate human flesh when available, which

they salted and dried. These farmers lived in a fortified town they called Lampiri.

Ayolas tried to established friendly relations with the Carios at first. But when that failed, he attacked the town with 300 men. Although he lost 16 men in the fight, the Carios soon surrendered. Ayolas took the town on August 15, the Feast of the Assumption, so he named the settlement Asuncion. (Today it is the capital city of Paraguay.) Ayolas defended the town with a fort of stone and wood and remained there for six months. Then, leaving behind a small group of soldiers under the command of Martinez de Irala, he traveled north along the Parana to search for the legendary Native American kingdom.

The Paiembos people assured Ayolas that a fabulously rich kingdom was nearby. But as Ayolas entered the upper reaches of the Parana River, he and his men were ambushed and the entire company was killed. Irala stayed in command of the remote outpost of Asuncion for the next 30 years. When Jesuits established missions on the Parana to convert the native peoples, the Spanish and Native Americans began to mingle and intermarry. Eventually this resulted in the so-called mestizo (mixed European and Native American ancestry) population of modern Paraguay. Because of its remote location so far from easy communication with Spain, Asuncion declared independence from both Spain and Argentina early in South American history, on May 14–15, 1811.

The failed colony

Back in Buenos Aires, with no word from Ayolas, Mendoza feared that the expedition had failed. Increasingly debilitated by his disease, he decided to leave the suffering colony and return to Spain. The settlers he left behind held out through starvation and Native American attacks for the next five years and then journeyed upriver to join their fellow countrymen at Asuncion.

Buenos Aires was abandoned for almost 50 years. It would not be rediscovered until 1580 by Juan de Garay, who added Nuestra Senora (Our Lady) to the original name. This became shortened to Buenos Aires and the town became the capital of the United Provinces of the Rio de la Plata in 1816. It was named the federal capital of Argentina in 1880.

Pedro de Mendoza never returned to his native land. He died aboard his ship in the Atlantic Ocean on June 23, 1537. He was buried at sea.

Today, Buenos Aires is the capital of Argentina.

Chapter Seven
Francisco de Orellana
On the Amazon (1541)

South America's Amazon River is the second longest river in the world after the Nile, but it is the world's largest in terms of volume and the area of its drainage basin. The Amazon flows almost 4,000 miles (6,437 kilometers) from high in the Peruvian Andes to its mouth in the Atlantic Ocean in northeastern Brazil. About 25 percent of all the water that runs off the earth's surface is carried by this mighty river. Its mouth is about 10 times the size of the Mississippi's mouth, and the discharge at the mouth is so great that it dilutes the ocean water from salty to brackish (less salty) more than 150 miles (241 kilometers) offshore. It has more than 1,000 known tributaries. The Amazon's total drainage basin covers some 2,700,000 square miles (6,992,967 square kilometers), nearly twice the area drained by any other river in the world. The first European to travel this great river system of South America was Spanish adventurer Francisco de Orellana (c.1490–1546).

In the New World

Almost nothing is known of Orellana's early life except that he was born in Trujillo, Spain. He sailed to the West Indies in about 1527 and saw service in modern Nicaragua. A close friend or a

Francisco de Orellana (c.1490–1546)

relative of Francisco Pizarro, Orellana accompanied him on the expedition to Peru in 1530–1533. After the conquest, he moved to the coast of modern Ecuador, where he founded the city of Guayaquil and became its governor in 1538.

Two years later Pizarro's half-brother, Gonzalo, was instructed to find the so-called Land of Cinnamon, thought to be somewhere east of the modern-day

The Amazon basin is the largest river drainage basin in the world.

Ecuadorean capital of Quito. Orellana became lieutenant over a force that numbered 220 Spaniards and 4,000 Native Americans. Orellana was sent back to Guayaquil for a troop of horses. When he returned to Quito in February 1541, Pizarro had already left.

Orellana hurried after the main party, which he joined in March. However, by that time the entire expedition had suffered badly in the mountains from lack of provisions, and three-quarters of the Native Americans and 140 Spanish soldiers had either died or deserted.

To the river

At a point where the Coca River meets the Napo in eastern Peru, the men constructed a boat named the *San Pedro*. Orellana was instructed to set off downstream to find food. With a force of 50 soldiers, he arrived at a village on

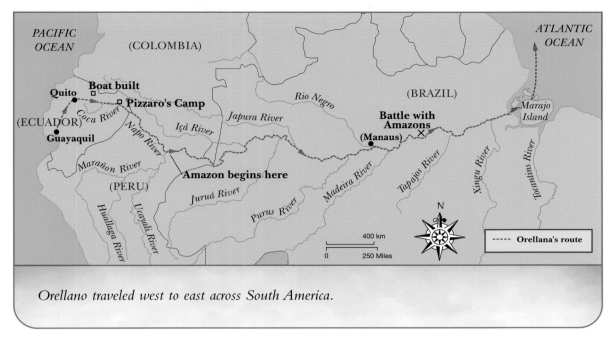

Orellano traveled west to east across South America.

the Napo but was unable to return upstream against the **current.** Instead he sent three men back to Pizarro and built a second boat, called the *Victoria,* to continue downstream on the Napo. In the meantime Pizarro, who was now down to 80 men, had decided to return to Quito by a more northerly route.

At a point where the Napo and Ucayali Rivers converge, it seemed impossible to return north. So Orellana unknowingly entered the great river system of South America. As he drifted downstream, he passed numerous tributaries, such as the river that Orellana named Rio Negro. However, the waters of the Negro are not really black (*negro* is Spanish for black) but a color more like dark tea. The color comes from large amounts

of partially decomposed organic matter. The large quantity of organic compounds is not filtered out by the sand, and the overload gives the water its dark color.

Besides the spectacular foliage and bird and animal life, encounters with Native Americans were frequent along the Amazon. Orellana and his men often fled for their lives. In one of the encounters at the junction of the Madeira River, he later claimed to have entered into a battle with warriorlike women. They reminded him of the legendary Amazons, a race of women warriors in Greek mythology. Such a race was never found, but the tales persist to this day. It is believed that the Amazon River was named by Orellana for the warriors he claimed to have met on his journey.

After stopping for a period of nearly three weeks to repair the boats, Orellana drifted to the mouth of the Amazon and the open sea on August 26, 1542. He was the first European on record to see and travel the length of the Amazon River.

Now the boats hugged the coast toward Guiana and finally reached Trinidad in September. From there, Orellana returned across the Atlantic, landing first in Portugal. The king was very gracious and offered to provide finances for a return trip to the Amazon. Although the Treaty of Tordesillas put the region of the Amazon in Spanish hands, the Portuguese saw the coast of Brazil as their own.

Hoping for greater gains from Spain, Orellana continued on to Valladolid in May 1543. After many months of fascinating, often exaggerated, tales of his expedition, Orellana got the backing he wanted. However, Spain could not give him ownership over the area since it was disputed with Portugal.

The tragic return

It took until May 11, 1545, for the expedition to sail out of Sanlucar. Some of the problems were financial and some

Rain forest covers the banks of this stretch of the Amazon River in Brazil.

had to do with Portuguese spies in the area. One of the problems was Orellana himself. He had decided to marry a young girl named Ana de Ayala, and was determined to take her and her sisters along on the voyage. After all those arrangements were made, Orellana left Sanlucar with four ships, 200 infantrymen, 100 horsemen, and tons of supplies. He was instructed to establish two towns, one on each side of the Amazon's mouth.

The voyage was a disaster. Three months were spent in the Canary Islands trying to get all the necessary supplies. By the time he arrived off the coast of Brazil in late December 1545, Orellana had lost two ships in the Atlantic, about half his crew, and eleven horses. They took refuge with friendly Native Americans, and Orellana and a small crew sailed upstream to find the main channel of the Amazon. Orellana's ship supposedly capsized and he died in November 1546. His young wife, along with about 40 survivors, were rescued from the delta area by a Spanish ship. The last heard of Ana de Ayala was that she was taken to Panama where she spent the rest of her life.

Marajo Island is formed by sediments deposited in the Amazon delta.

Chapter Eight

Francis Drake

Second Around the World (1577–1580)

A portrait shows Sir Francis Drake (c.1540–1596).

He was the greatest seaman of the Elizabethan Age and its most renowned pirate. A favorite of Elizabeth I, who knighted him in 1580, Sir Francis Drake (c.1540–1596) became the hero of the British Empire, the second voyager and first Englishman around the world. Although his was the second circumnavigation of the globe, he was the first navigator to complete the journey. Magellan did not live to finish what was the first around-the-world voyage (1519–1521), although his ship successfully returned to England. Drake added to his glory in 1588 by leading England to victory over the Spanish Armada, which marked the beginning of a long era of British sea power.

A Devonshire lad

Drake was the son of a tenant farmer in Devonshire on the Crowndale estate of Lord Francis Russell, second earl of Bedford. Born around 1540, he was the oldest of twelve boys. His father was an ardent Protestant lay preacher. A violent pro-Catholic uprising when Drake was about seven years old forced the family to flee to Kent in southeastern England. It left Drake with a lasting hatred of Catholics, which would influence his career.

Had Drake stayed in Devonshire, he would probably have become a farmer like his father. Instead, like many other poor boys, he took to the sea when he was about thirteen. He was apprenticed on a small coastal vessel that called at North Sea ports. Sailing one of the harshest stretches of water in the world sharpened Drake's navigational skills. When the old sea captain died, Drake inherited his boat at an early age.

But Drake had higher adventure in mind than the North Sea. Luckily for him, he also had a wealthy relative in John Hawkins, a merchant seaman from Plymouth. The powerful Hawkins family was just beginning a trade route to the so-called New World. This was the New World that Pope Alexander VI had given to England's enemy, Spain; a fact that Drake never forgot or forgave. Now 23 years old and dissatisfied with the coastal trade, Drake sold his boat and joined the Hawkins family's fleet.

To the West Indies

For a while Drake was a purser, a sort of record keeper, on voyages to northern Spain and the western coast of Africa. Then he joined the Hawkins trade triangle. These were voyages from England to western Africa to pick up slaves to be traded for tobacco, sugar, cotton, and other goods in the West Indies to take back to Europe. During these voyages, Drake saw firsthand the way the Spanish treated foreigners who ventured into their territories. His cargoes were seized. On his second voyage to the West Indies with John Hawkins in 1566, the English ships were attacked by the Spanish. Many of the crew were killed at San Juan de Ulua, which is near present-day Veracruz, Mexico.

Drake returned to England in command of the vessel *Judith*, which, along with a ship led by Hawkins, had survived the attack. More than ever he was determined to have revenge on the Spanish and the Spanish king, Philip II. Although Drake was a hero when he returned to England, the expedition was a financial disaster. Nevertheless, Drake had proven himself to be an outstanding seaman.

A pirate's life

Drake's heroism was not lost on Queen Elizabeth I. Nor was his desire to get revenge on the Spanish. He obtained a privateering license from the queen. This amounted to permission to steal from any ship, but especially from Spain. The technical difference was that a so-called pirate operated on his own, but a privateer had the authority of government behind him and was entitled to a share of the proceeds. In other words their work was the same, but a pirate was outside the law, while a privateer was within the law.

Privateer Drake set sail for America in 1572 with great ambitions. In command of the 70-ton *Pasha* and 25-ton *Swan*, he cruised the northern coast of Panama and sacked the important town of Nombre de Dios (Name of God), near Portobello, where Spain stored its captured Peruvian gold. The gold was taken across Panama from west to east for further shipment to Europe. Drake was wounded in the attack, but that was a small matter compared to the enormous amount of gold and silver he captured. It made the tenant farmer's son a very wealthy man.

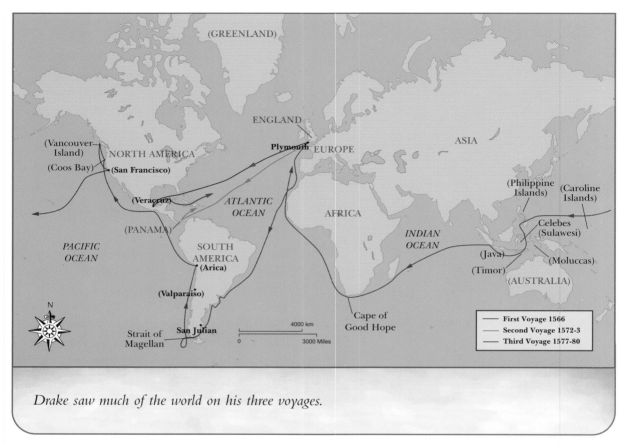

Drake saw much of the world on his three voyages.

Flushed with success, Drake sailed on to a spot where he could anchor. Then he traveled across the isthmus of Panama. He stood on a high ridge of land and stared at the Pacific Ocean, which so far had been barred to all but the Spanish. Drake dedicated his life then and there to "sail an English ship in these seas."

Francis Drake returned to England on August 9, 1573, a rich and famous man. He bought a house in Plymouth and offered his services to the queen. Unfortunately for Drake's continuing plans of revenge, the queen and Philip II of Spain had come to a peaceful accord, at least for the time being. Not wanting to upset the delicate balance between the two countries, the queen decided not to send Drake back to the West Indies. Instead, she asked him to go to Ireland where the Earl of Essex was trying to put down a rebellion.

Secretly, Elizabeth was delighted with Drake's pursuit of the Spanish even if she could not openly say so. Drake wisely realized that this was not the right time to press the issue. So he

A painting shows Spanish treasure ships being seized by Francis Drake's fleet.

Now the timing was right. Once again, relations with Spain were declining. Elizabeth gave her approval. It was perfect for Drake. He could do maximum damage to Spain while benefiting the Queen, his country, and himself. For the first time, Drake met face-to-face with his queen and heard her say that she would be happy to have revenge upon the king of Spain for injuries suffered. It was her official command.

The journey begins

Drake gathered a fleet of only five ships. This would seem rather small when setting out to challenge what was the world's most powerful empire at the time. The ships and crew of fewer than 200 men, however, were well armed for the task. Drake's **flagship** was the 100-ton (91-metric ton) *Pelican*. They set out from Plymouth, England, on December 13, 1577.

Perhaps fearing dissension among the crew from the beginning, Drake said they were headed for Egypt and promised great riches. Only Drake, Captain John Winter, and Thomas Doughty, who knew Drake from the Ireland campaign, were aware of the true destination. But when the fleet passed Gibraltar and kept heading southwest, it was obvious they were not going to Egypt.

By the time the fleet reached Brazil in April 1578, Drake believed that Doughty was plotting a mutiny against him. The men were insecure and restless, egged

sailed to Ireland with a small squadron just as the queen had asked.

The time is right

Drake could not pursue his dream until 1577. What he proposed was a voyage to the South Seas through the **Strait** of Magellan at the tip of South America, something no Englishman had done. Officially, he would set up trading posts along the Pacific and explore an unknown continent rumored to lie far away in the South Pacific. What he really wanted to do was attack Spanish settlements along the western coast of South America.

on by Doughty. Never one to have his command questioned, when the fleet stopped at San Julian, Drake had Doughty tried and executed. Drake had no more trouble from the crew.

To the Pacific

On August 21, 1578, Drake reached the **Strait** of Magellan at the southern tip of South America. Now he changed the name of his flagship to *The Golden Hind*, in honor of an early patron whose coat of arms bore a deer. Then he destroyed two of his five ships, transferring their provisions to the other three. He calculated that it would be easier to keep three ships together through the **strait** than five.

It took sixteen days to sail through the perilous strait, buffeted by winds and bitter driving rain. Magellan had taken more than a month for passage. Now from the deck of a ship, Drake saw the Pacific Ocean for the second time. Both good and bad fortune occurred in sailing the strait. Drake's own ship was blown off course to about 100 miles (161 kilometers) south of Tierra del Fuego, the southernmost tip of the continent. Without intending to, Drake had shown that the land south of the strait was not a continent but a continuation of South America. The bad fortune was that Drake lost one of his ships in the passage and was separated from his second in command in the *Elizabeth*. When the two ships did not meet at a rendezvous point, the captain of the

Drake's ship, the Golden Hind, *was once named* Pelican.

Elizabeth, believing that the *Hind* had sunk, sailed for England in November. Of the five-ship fleet that had begun the journey around the world, only the **flagship** remained.

Once in the Pacific, Drake sailed up the coast of South America on his true mission. He passed safely along the coast like a whirlwind. The Spanish left their territories unguarded, never dreaming a hostile ship would appear in these waters. Drake raided outposts in present-day Chile and Peru and

captured a Spanish merchant ship at Valparaiso. Before long, the *Hind* was low in the water, loaded with bars of gold and silver, minted Spanish coins, and precious stones.

After Valparaiso word spread quickly of the English pirate, and Drake found it hard to surprise an outpost and get away with the loot. But before setting out westward, he sailed north probably as far as Vancouver Island, British Columbia. Drake became the first European to see the west coast of Canada. He thought of looking for a Northwest Passage back to England, but bitter weather sent him south again. In June 1579 he stopped near present-day Coos Bay, Oregon, and on June 17, he anchored north of present-day San Francisco in what is now known as Drake's Bay to make repairs on the *Hind*. Drake named the area New Albion and took possession of it for the queen of England.

At this time he met Miwok people in the area, who threatened the crew with arrows when they saw the shipbuilding repairs on the beach. But Drake did not overreact and was able to convince the Miwok that he had come in peace. On July 23 they departed on friendly terms. Now Drake turned his sails west across the Pacific. He and his crew would not see land again for 68 days.

To the South Pacific

After more than two months at sea, the Drake expedition spotted land. It was probably the Palau group in the Carolines Islands. In contrast to their experience with the Miwoks, the crew had to fire shots into the water to keep the native islanders from boarding the ship. Several islanders were killed. From there Drake sailed to the Philippines and then the Moluccas, where he was generally well-received and apparently arranged a treaty that gave the English the right to trade for spices. After a stop in present-day Indonesia, the *Golden Hind* ran aground and had to be repaired. Drake was an excellent deep-sea navigator, but these waters were treacherous and totally uncharted, and he had struck a reef.

A month was spent in Celebes (now Sulawesi) for repairs. For a time, he considered sailing on to Cathay (China), but decided the risk for his crew was too great. Instead, after stops at Timor and Java, Drake set his course across the Indian Ocean and the **Cape** of Good Hope in March 1580. He rounded the Cape in June.

The victorious captain

On September 26, 1580, Drake and the heavily laden *Golden Hind* sailed into Plymouth Harbor, England. Only 56 members of the original crew survived. They had all been at sea for two years and ten months.

Francis Drake was a hero and a fabulously wealthy man. The cargo of treasure and spices with which he

Queen Elizabeth I of England knights Francis Drake aboard his ship.

returned was estimated, in today's prices, at about $10 million. His fortune and his reputation were secure. He was hailed as leading the second successful journey around the world and was the first Englishman to sail the Pacific, the Indian, and the South Atlantic Oceans.

It seems that the only people not happy with Drake were the Spanish. In fact, the Spanish king was furious. He protested Drake's pirate-like conduct in Spanish imperial waters. At first this protest made Queen Elizabeth hesitant to acknowledge Drake's feat.

However, in January 1581, with the *Golden Hind* anchored at Deptford in the Thames **Estuary,** the queen herself came aboard to knight him for his great accomplishment. The tenant farmer's son was now Sir Francis. The queen also made plans to preserve the *Golden Hind*.

That same year, Drake became the mayor of Plymouth, a post he fulfilled with as much efficiency as his expeditions

at sea. He organized a water supply for the city that lasted 300 years.

Drake's wife, a Cornish woman named Mary Newman whom he had married in 1569, died in 1583. Two years later he married Elizabeth Sydenham, an heiress and daughter of a Devonshire businessman. To fit his new status, Drake bought a stylish country home near Plymouth. Called Buckland Abbey, it is now a national museum.

Interestingly enough, Drake had to have someone else buy the Abbey for him from owner Sir Richard Grenville, a naval commander. Grenville would never have sold the estate if he knew that Drake was buying it. Francis Drake was a great hero to the people and even to the queen, but not to the well-born Englishmen of his day. Despite his accomplishments, they considered him an upstart. He was rich but without the background and breeding of the gentry. And certainly without the manners, grace, and accent of the so-called West Country people. Explorer Sir Martin Frosbisher, for instance, disliked Drake intensely. If Drake cared about his status with the English gentry, he gave no sign of it. It was enough that he was in excellent standing with the queen.

Once more a hero

In 1585 the queen sent Drake back to sea in command of 25 ships. His mission was the same: Cause as much damage to the Spanish as possible. Hostilities had broken out between the two countries once more.

First, Drake attacked Vigo, Spain, and then crossed the Atlantic to the West Indies. He captured Santiago on the southeastern coast of Cuba. Then he plundered the cities of Cartagena in Colombia, Santo Domingo (Hispaniola), and St. Augustine in Florida. He also sailed as far north as present-day North Carolina.

Elizabeth I could not have picked a better man for the job. He caused so much damage to Spanish holdings that the Bank of Spain went broke and the renowned German bank of Augsburg denied more credit to the Spanish king. This caused even the queen's ministers, who also disapproved of Drake and his methods, to admit that he was their best weapon against the Spanish.

The defeat of the Spanish Armada

Philip II of Spain had had enough. For some time it was known that he was preparing an armada to attack and capture the "heretic" British Isles. During the reign of the queen's father, Henry VIII, England had officially broken ties with the Catholic Church. Therefore, Pope Sixtus V readily agreed with Spain's plan, called "The Enterprise of England." Once word of the planned attack reached her, Queen Elizabeth gave Drake complete freedom to do whatever he could to destroy Spanish power.

Drake proceeded to do just that. In 1587, with a fleet of 30 ships, he sailed to the Bay of Cadiz near Spanish-held Gilbraltar and attacked Spanish ships. In just 36 hours he destroyed thousands of tons of supplies and shipping, all destined to join the armada. Drake laughingly said that he was "singeing the king of Spain's beard." It is estimated that Drake's actions delayed the sailing of the Spanish Armada by about a year.

But Spain was not to be defeated so easily. By late July 1588, the fleet of about 130 ships, 8,000 seaman, and perhaps 19,000 soldiers sailed into the English Channel. The Spanish king called the armada "invincible."

The English fleet was smaller, sometimes during the fighting numbering about 100 ships. The vessels carried fewer crew than the Spanish but were better armed. The fleet was commanded by Charles Howard, 2nd Baron Howard of Effingham. His second in command was Sir Francis Drake.

It was Drake's enthusiasm throughout the fight, which lasted until August 9, that played heavily in the defeat of the supposedly invincible Spanish Armada. Only 60 ships returned to Spain. As many as 15,000 Spanish died in the battle. England suffered relatively few casualties.

With the defeat of the Spanish Armada, England was saved from invasion and the prestige of the greatest European power of the age was dealt a near-fatal blow. It also marked the beginning of England's long domination of the oceans.

The hero retires

Once again Francis Drake was England's hero. He was immortalized in poems and with an endless stream of souvenirs. He returned to Plymouth, but he was not finished sailing. In 1596 he sailed to the West Indies with John Hawkins. The mission was to capture Spanish settlements there. This attempt was a failure, largely because so much of the crew fell ill with dysentery, an acute intestinal disorder. Drake himself became a victim. He was buried at sea near Puerto Bello (Portobelo, Panama) on January 28, 1596.

Sir Francis Drake was the hero of Elizabethan England and one of the world's greatest seamen. Daring, bold, and ruthless, he embodied the spirit of the adventurer, an explorer whose voyages were important and wide ranging. English people adored this mariner, and others feared him. To historians, he was more skillful in navigation than any other, but to his enemy, the Spanish, he remained "the master thief of the unknown world."

Epilogue:

What Did They Find?

The story of exploration in South America is primarily the story of Spanish conquest in the New World. From men such as Vespucci, the first European to realize what he had come upon, to Pizarro who conquered Peru and destroyed an entire native civilization, to Orellana who sailed the great river, Spanish claims and conquests brought that nation to the height of its power in the 1500s. But Spain was constantly challenged during this period by the Portuguese, who with men such as Cabral also staked their claim to the riches of this previously unknown and enormous land. The English, who would find their power and glory in the northern continent, involved themselves to the south with the voyage of Sir Francis Drake.

With the exception of Drake, the explorers in this book left their mark on the continent of South America and changed its history in very profound and lasting ways. Spanish and Portuguese names and customs remain, intermixed with the customs of the Native Americans. The flavor and history of these peoples are forever entwined with the two major sea powers of centuries ago.

The explorers in this book were not interested in leaving their mark on history. For most of them, it was the promise of gold, wealth, and power that lured them and kept them going during their difficult journeys. They were all brave men but, for the most part, not noble men. They had little sense of justice and fairness. But in the 1500s and the world of the conquistadors, "might makes right" was not just an idle saying. They lived the only way they knew how to live and fought in that way, too. Perhaps it is that willingness of the early explorers to face any danger for their own desired goals that fascinates us even to this day.

Important Events in the Exploration of the South America

1499	Vespucci makes voyage to South America, sees mouth of the Amazon River
1500	Cabral leaves on voyage to India but lands in Brazil; Vespucci makes second voyage to South America; reaches Brazil and harbor of Rio de Janeiro
1503–04	Vespucci claims a last voyage to New World, doubted by historians
1507	Waldseemuller puts Vespucci's name on New World maps as discoverer
1508	Solis sails to Central America, explores Mexico and Nicaragua
1509	Pizarro joins expedition to Colombia, Central America
1514	Solis makes second voyage to Central America
1516	Solis is first European to enter mouth of the Rio de la Plata, explores Uruguay
1519	Magellan leaves on first around-the-world voyage, September 20
1520	Magellan reaches Rio de la Plata; sights Pacific Ocean November 27
1521	Magellan dies in battle on island of Mactan, Philippines, April 21
1522	Last ship of Magellan's voyage returns home to Spain
1523	Pizarro begins journey in conquest of Incas; expedition fails
1526	Pizarro begins second expedition to the Incas; reaches Peru
1531	Pizarro's third expedition in search of the Inca Empire
1532	Pizarro captures chief of the Incas and puts him to death; enters Incan city of Cuzco
1535	Pizarro founds capital city of Lima, Peru; Mendoza sails to South America, founds Buenos Aires, Argentina, August 24; deputy Ayolas founds Asuncion, Paraguay
1541	Pizarro is assassinated in his palace in Lima; Orellana explores the Amazon river from Ecuador to its mouth
1545	Orellana makes second voyage to the Amazon region
1572	Drake sails to Panama, sees Pacific Ocean
1577	Drake begins around-the-world voyage
1580	Drake returns from voyage September 26, second person and first Englishman to sail around the world
1585	Drake attacks Spanish holdings in the West Indies

Glossary

adobe building material made of sun-dried brick or straw

caravel small sailing ship of the 1400s and 1500s

cape point of land jutting out into the water

cask barrel-shaped container, usually for liquids

circumference outside boundary of a circle

clove bud of a tropical tree used as spice and for oil

current part of a body of water that moves continuously in one direction

dynasty succession of rulers in the same line, or powerful group or family that maintains a position for a long time

estuary arm of the sea at the lower end of a river

flagship ship of the fleet that carries the commander

founder one who establishes something, usually an organization, a nation, or a city

heathen one who does not acknowledge a particular religion

landmark object on land that can serve as a marker

page youth in the service of a person of rank

peninsula piece of land nearly surrounded by water and connected to the mainland

pillage act of looting or plundering

proclamation official formal public announcement

quinine bitter extract from cinchona bark used in medicine as treatment for malaria

smallpox contagious disease characterized by skin eruptions and scar formation

strait narrow passageway connecting two large bodies of water

viceroy governor of a country or province as representative of the king

whirlpool water moving rapidly in a circle, producing a depression that draws in objects

Further Reading

Baker, Daniel B. (ed.). *Explorers and Discovers of the World*. Detroit: Gale, 1993.

Bergen, Lara Rice. *The Travels of Francisco Pizarro*. Chicago: Raintree, 2000.

Bohlander, Richard E. (ed.). *World Explorers and Discoverers*. Cambridge, Mass.: Da Capo, 2003.

Champion, Neil. *Sir Francis Drake*. Chicago: Heinemann, 2002.

Ray, Kurt. *Amerigo Vespucci: Italian Explorer of the Americas*. New York: Rosen, 2002.

Reid, Struan. *Groundbreakers: Ferdinand Magellan*. Chicago: Heinemann, 2002.

Index